DIGITAL AND INFORMATION LITERACY ™

MANAGING YOUR DIGITAL FOOTPRINT

ROBERT GRAYSON

rosen publishing's
rosen
central®

New York

Published in 2011 by The Rosen Publishing Group, Inc.
29 East 21st Street, New York, NY 10010

Copyright © 2011 by The Rosen Publishing Group, Inc.

First Edition

Library of Congress Cataloging-in-Publication Data

Grayson, Robert, 1951–
Managing your digital footprint / Robert Grayson. — 1st ed.
    p. cm. — (Digital and information literacy)
Includes bibliographical references and index.
ISBN 978-1-4488-1319-3 (library binding)
ISBN 978-1-4488-2290-4 (pbk.)
ISBN 978-1-4488-2296-6 (6-pack)
1. Internet—Social aspects—Juvenile literature. 2. Internet—Safety measures—Juvenile literature. 3. Online etiquette—Juvenile literature. 4. Privacy, Right of—Juvenile literature. 5. Youth—Conduct of life—Juvenile literature. I. Title.
HM851.G73 2011
004.67'8—dc22

2010025746

Manufactured in the United States of America

CPSIA Compliance Information: Batch #W11YA: For further information, contact Rosen Publishing, New York, New York, at 1-800-237-9932.

CONTENTS

INTRODUCTION

Privacy is valuable, and a good reputation is priceless. A person's "digital footprint"—or the content about a person found in cyberspace—plays a major role in both of these vital areas.

In today's digital environment, everything that is written, viewed, posted, or sent becomes part of a permanent record. As a result, people must think about the best way to manage their digital footprint. Individuals need to do everything possible to ensure that this digital recording of life reflects positively on them.

People put a great deal of thought into their personal appearance, hairstyle, clothes, even the colors that make them look their best. Now the same amount of care must be put into one's digital appearance and the components that make up one's digital footprint. Is that footprint appealing? Is it accurate? Will it be a source of great pride later on? Will it be held in high regard by future generations?

A digital footprint is built throughout a lifetime, just like a person's reputation. For young people today, the elements that shape a digital footprint begin falling into place right now. The way people are portrayed through a digital footprint can have an impact on which colleges they get into and what jobs they are offered. It can shape the opinions people have about

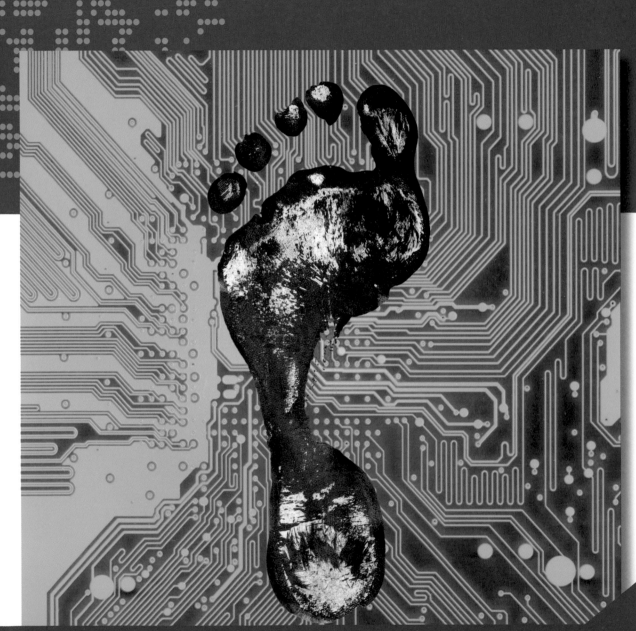

Consider the digital footprint: it is more telling than a fingerprint and more revealing than DNA. It is the makeup of a person's digital identity.

others before even meeting them and influence whether people want to get together in the first place.

Never before have people had the ability to communicate so easily with so many others around the world and to leave behind such a rich recorded history. This creates many opportunities but also some dangers.

Individuals do not have complete control over everything that makes up their digital footprint. However, there are key aspects of this digital DNA that people can manage. To the extent that it is within their power, people have to take an active role in developing a positive digital footprint.

Just as there is appropriate behavior in all walks of life, there is appropriate behavior in the digital universe. When people had less technology, impolite, uncivil, or embarrassing behavior could be lost in the shuffle, never to be brought up again. In a society of paper files, records could be lost—sometimes destroyed on purpose—and that destruction left no trace. By contrast, in this digital era, a person's online travels can be reconstructed through the aid of computer backup systems and traces left behind by digital tracks. That makes a digital footprint a very powerful tool that no one can underestimate.

Like fingerprints and DNA, a digital footprint is proof of a person's involvement in some activity. Keeping that in mind, people have a measure of control over what their digital footprint says about them. That control must be used wisely.

Chapter 1

What Is a Digital Footprint?

hances are, a baby born today already enters the world with a digital footprint. When the fetus is a few months old, a sonogram will be taken. The proud parents can e-mail the image of the unborn child to relatives and friends. Those people can send it on to others. While still in the womb, the baby already has an online presence. By the time the child goes to college, he or she will have thousands of interactions online and will leave behind many more digital artifacts.

A Digital Trail

Everything done in cyberspace leaves a trail. In the days before the Internet, the accumulation of records about a person was referred to as a paper trail. The big difference between paper and digital trails is that tracks left in cyberspace are extremely difficult to destroy. Written, photographic, audio, or video content of any kind about a person that finds its way into cyberspace forms that person's digital footprint. Unlike footprints in the sand, a digital footprint cannot simply be washed away.

Paper documents can be shredded, burned, ripped up, or thrown in the garbage. If a copy was never made, the document is gone forever. In the digital world, once something appears online, it can be passed from one person to another and posted in other places without permission. It will probably remain somewhere online forever and may pop up unexpectedly during a routine search.

Whatever people do in cyberspace becomes part of their digital footprint. Blogs, photos uploaded to sites like Flickr, e-mails, text messages, videos posted on YouTube, calls and messaging on Skype, posts on Facebook walls, offhand comments in chat rooms or newsgroups, and other online activities all combine to create this revealing digital footprint. Also included is any information people post about themselves in their profiles on social networking sites such as Facebook, MySpace, Google Buzz, Buzznet, Bebo, and myYearbook. Cell phone communication is part of a digital footprint, as is activity that takes place on personal digital assistants (PDAs),

It seems innocent enough, but every time people visit Facebook, MySpace, or any Web site, they are adding to their digital footprint, and their online activity can be tracked.

iPads, and smartphones. A digital footprint can even include information captured by a global positioning system (GPS) used to get directions.

Anyone who has ever done research online knows how much outdated information appears on the Internet—data that is never deleted and easily found. The danger occurs when that information could harm a person's reputation—such as embarrassing photographs, unfounded statements, private writings, rants, or even incriminating e-mails or text messages. This kind of information can come up in a search and have negative consequences for a long time to come. For example, material found online may prompt prospective employers not to hire otherwise qualified candidates.

From Private to Public

Looking into a job applicant's online persona is becoming routine among hiring managers, especially since it is so easy to do. In a study by the popular job site CareerBuilder.com, 26 percent of hiring managers said they had checked a job seeker's digital footprint. Of the hiring managers who admitted making these checks, 63 percent said they found something that made them decide not to offer a job to an applicant. Twenty-six percent of college admissions officers also said they searched the Internet for information about students applying to their colleges, according to a study by the University of Massachusetts's Center for Market Research. With both employers and colleges checking into a person's digital footprint, having an unblemished record in cyberspace is extremely important.

People also leave tracks every time they visit a Web site. Most people are not even aware of the data trails they leave. A computer's Web browser records all the sites visited by users of that computer. Text files, known as cookies, collect and store information about users on the hard drive of a computer. Sometimes these cookies contain sensitive information, like passwords or account information, embedded within them. Computer forensic experts can determine a great deal by looking at the Web searches people do. A person's search habits can reveal financial needs, shopping trends, career choices, hobbies, or vacation plans.

Today, people's online personas can come into play when they apply for jobs or for college admission. Many recruiters are checking out applicants' online activity and questioning them about it.

Every time people buy something online, they provide names, credit card information, phone numbers, and addresses. E-commerce sites record this information to put together in-depth customer profiles. These profiles prompt individual sites to offer customers merchandise they might be interested in. This information also becomes part of a person's overall digital footprint. Additional information is gathered while a person is doing online banking, filling out job applications, completing online surveys, and getting price estimates for insurance.

File   Edit   View   Favorites   Tools   Help

A VALUABLE LESSON

A Valuable Lesson

It takes time for people to learn exactly how new communication technologies work and the impact mistakes can have. When Salisbury University president Janet Dudley-Eshbach posted some family vacation photos on her Facebook page in 2007, with captions that some found offensive, it created quite a stir.

Dudley-Eshbach had posted the photos in good fun and thought that only a small circle of friends would see them. "My understanding was that, with my privacy settings in Facebook, my page could be viewed only by those to whom I granted access," she told the *Chronicle of Higher Education*. Somehow the pictures traveled beyond those limits.

In a statement released through the university's media relations department, the president said, "Many of us are learning about the positives and negatives of public networking sites, such as Facebook." Dudley-Eshbach removed her Facebook profile and apologized for the misjudgment. The incident fueled debate over whether there can be any expectation of privacy in cyberspace.

Cell Phone Tracks

Digital tracks can be traced even further. Few of the nearly three hundred million cell phone users in the United States realize that there are small GPS devices in many phones. The way phones are routed through towers helps cell phone companies keep track of everywhere a customer goes with a particular phone. Called location logs, these GPS systems are not readily visible to users. Law enforcement officials have been relying on them more and more to help with criminal investigations.

Even more ingenious, the FBI has developed a way to activate a criminal suspect's cell phone from a remote location and turn the phone into a listening device. Perhaps the phone is off, sitting in someone's pocket. FBI officials can activate that phone remotely, without the user's knowledge. Then they can turn it into a microphone to eavesdrop on conversations people are having in their homes, offices, or public places. The only defense against this new form of surveillance that, so far, has been ruled legal by U.S. courts, is to take the battery out of the phone when it is not in use.

Discovering flaws in the latest phone technology is nothing new. When party line phones were first developed in the early twentieth century, people soon realized that they had to be careful about what they said, as others were listening and gossip would follow.

Not-So-Casual Communications

The digital world of text messages, tweets, and e-mails seems as if it is a casual means of communication. It is likened to a telephone conversation or even a relaxed exchange in someone's backyard. Generally speaking, however, when people communicate by phone or over the backyard fence, no one is keeping a permanent record of what is being said. But when a digital device is involved, a record is made.

In the professional world, people have long talked and joked casually "around the water cooler." Today, however, people have lost their jobs over private comments they made to coworkers in e-mails or text messages that they never thought would leak out to others, especially their superiors in the workplace.

Similarly, many public figures have suffered the embarrassment of having private e-mails or texts publicly released. Comments like those in the e-mails or texts would probably never have been made in formal written

Texting is fast, simple, and convenient, but it leaves a permanent trail. Taking the time to think about your message before pressing the "send" button is well worth the effort.

letters. Why? People think carefully about what they put in letters, which they know are likely to become part of a permanent record somewhere. They consider how a letter reflects on them and the person or issue they are writing about. They know their letters can be made public and that people in authority might read them and take action based on them. Nothing would be put into a letter that the author would not want anyone else to see.

Franklin Twp. Public Library
1584 Coles Mill Road
Franklinville, NJ 08322-

But in casual digital communications, people often write things off the top of their heads. In the heat of the moment, they may write e-mails to a close friend, classmate, or coworker, calling others nasty names or spreading unfounded gossip—all because they think these communications are private. A person who gets an e-mail message can forward it to others or make it public without the sender's knowledge. With a little work, even an unsigned e-mail or text can be traced back to its original sender. Unflattering or untruthful comments, made in anger in digital communications, can come back to haunt the author years after the messages are sent.

Today, communication is simpler, faster, and more wide-ranging than ever before. However, people need to take greater responsibility in order to handle these opportunities. This makes managing a digital footprint a very important skill.

→ Chapter 2

Put Your Best Foot Forward

The digital world certainly has its pitfalls, so successfully navigating it calls for shrewdness and savvy. But when used properly, powerful digital media can open up an array of limitless possibilities. In this world, amazing achievements, even by one person, can have a global impact.

A Worldwide Platform

Digital communication technology has given everyone a new, potentially worldwide audience. For example, a person might create a blog, or online journal, about natural pet care for just a few friends to read. Suddenly, that blog can be transmitted to pet lovers across the world who are interested in the subject. Faraway readers can comment on the blog and ask questions. The author can respond and might be encouraged to share additional insights on natural pet care by writing more entries. People with an interest in natural health care for pets may then decide to form a network to exchange information about the key points raised in the blog.

The blog author's thoughtful commentary and creative ideas will become part of a digital footprint. In the future, the blogger may use it to present her work to potential employers or college admissions officers.

It can reveal another side or hidden talent that might otherwise be concealed in a world without a digital platform.

The same is true of creative pursuits in the world of music, film, literature, and art. Today, people can take work they are proud of and present it to the world without having to go through an agent, record producer, publisher, or distributor. Creative people literally have open access to a world stage.

The digital footprint of Julie Powell loomed large in a very positive way. In August 2002 she started a blog that documented her attempt to make all the recipes in Julia Child's classic cookbook *Mastering the Art of French Cooking*. The goal was to make all 524 recipes in the book over the course of one year.

Julie Powell captured the nation's attention with her imaginative blog about her culinary adventures. Her accounts of re-creating 524 of Julia Child's recipes in one year became a book and a hit movie.

The effort would probably never have gotten under way if Powell had no one to tell about her day-to-day trials and tribulations, as well as followers to cheer her on. That could only be accomplished through digital communication, which both showcased and recorded her kitchen adventures. The blog had a small following at first but then picked up an avid fan base. The blog led to a book deal and a major movie, *Julie & Julia*, starring Amy Adams and Meryl Streep.

File   Edit   View   Favorites   Tools   Help

CRAFTING AN ONLINE PORTFOLIO

Crafting an Online Portfolio

The Internet provides many opportunities for creative people to save and share their work. In order for online work to be judged properly and fairly, it must be presented professionally. Proper spelling, punctuation, and grammar are essential when presenting written work. Any accompanying photos must be clear and in good taste.

By the same token, musical productions should have an air of professionalism when put online. They have to be planned properly, look and sound sharp, and be simple to download. Like record demos of years ago, an artist or group's early productions should be put together to showcase the talent of the creators.

These digital productions can serve as a portfolio or archive for those who created them. While the pieces may be raw and lack polish, they should be done tastefully and serve as positive promotional pieces.

These elements of a digital footprint can help to track an individual's personal and creative growth. As people hone their talents, it will show in their creative pursuits. The work will get better and better, and the digital artifacts will be the yardstick by which others measure that growth.

Too Much Information

While the World Wide Web has opened up new venues for creativity, it has also pierced the expectation of privacy. No matter how technically advanced communication gets, there are still some things that should remain private and not the subject of online conversations, blogs, or social networking sites.

There is no guarantee of privacy online: when conversations, opinions, and photographs are put online, they are there for everyone to see. The Internet cannot be confused with another creative tool, a handwritten diary. With a paper diary, people can record their most private thoughts and then keep the diary under lock and key in a dresser drawer. E-mails, text messages, and blog posts have a way of becoming public, even if that does not happen right after they are sent or posted. These digital writings, which the author might think of as private communications and closed to the world, are difficult if not impossible to eliminate from cyberspace. Long forgotten text messages, e-mails, and posts can resurface and cause tense, if not outright embarrassing, moments for the writer. These writings become a permanent part of a person's digital footprint, along with any photographs and videos associated with them.

The same attention that goes into creative endeavors intended for a wide audience has to be paid to even the most casual communications in the digital world. Before posting an item or e-mailing anything, a person has to ask: If this post or e-mail were accidentally released to the public, would it leave a bad impression of me? Some experts have recommended giving an item the "grandparent test." Ask yourself: Would I be proud or embarrassed if my grandparents were to see this? Sad as it may be, bad impressions travel faster than good ones and can do substantial damage.

No Expectation of Privacy

Consider the case of Cynthia Moreno. Her family had to move out of their hometown of Coalinga, California, in 2005 after Moreno, then a college

There is no guarantee of privacy when communicating in the digital world. Digital communications can travel much farther and faster than handwritten notes on paper.

student, made some unflattering statements about the town on her MySpace page. The family received death threats, and people stopped doing business with Moreno's father, which seriously hurt the family's income. The blog post was intended for just a few people to see and was posted for only six days. However, Roger Campbell, Moreno's former principal at Coalinga High School, read the post. Campbell sent the piece on to the *Coalinga Record*, a local newspaper, which published it and named Cynthia Moreno as the author.

File   Edit   View   Favorites   Tools   Help

BLOGGING TIPS

Blogging Tips

Starting a blog is a great way for young writers to practice their craft and share their work with others. Follow these tips so that a blog helps, rather than harms, your digital footprint.

- Keep blog entries fun, light, and on popular subjects.
- Be creative, but stay on topic.
- Avoid divulging personal information.
- Show your best side by using proper spelling, grammar, and punctuation.
- Steer clear of offensive language and rants.
- If someone makes an inappropriate comment on your blog, do not respond. Delete the comment. If necessary, block the person from commenting in the future.
- Set up your blog so that it is password-protected. Only people with whom you have shared the password will be able to read the blog. Ask a parent, teacher, or librarian for help with the setup.

Town residents were enraged by Moreno's rant about hating the town and lashed out at the entire family, which included a younger sister. The Moreno family sued the principal, the school district, and the newspaper, claiming, among other things, invasion of privacy. The California Fifth District Court of Appeals ruled against the Morenos in 2009. The court held that because Cynthia Moreno posted her comments on a MySpace blog, what she wrote was available for anyone with a computer to read. In doing so, she knowingly put the material in the public eye. With that in

Digital communications can be fun, light, and informative without getting personal. Avoid making mean-spirited or embarrassing comments that will hurt others and you. Keep the tone upbeat and positive.

mind, the court went on to rule that Moreno should have had no expectation of privacy.

The lesson to be learned from Cynthia Moreno and Julie Powell is this: When you go online you are never alone. For better or for worse, anything posted in cyberspace can go viral.

MYTHS & FACTS

MYTH When people die, their online presence dies with them.

FACT In cyberspace, an online presence never dies. Tributes and remembrances add to a digital footprint even after a person has passed away, giving future generations a glimpse of that person's life.

MYTH There is no information in a teenager's online profile that a hacker can use.

FACT If the profile includes a person's real name, address, phone number, date of birth, parents' names, and other relevant information, a hacker can use it to set up credit card accounts and other types of accounts long before the real person gets a chance to do so. Many victims of this kind of identity theft do not discover it until they try to obtain credit.

MYTH Freedom of speech means people can write or say whatever they want on the Internet and nobody can do anything about it.

FACT People have been sued, charged with crimes, fired from jobs, denied entry into college, and shunned by others for things they have said or done online. People may feel they have a right to say or do anything they want online, but that does not mean there are no consequences.

Chapter 3

Casual Communications, Serious Consequences

Today, people are encouraged to reveal all kinds of data about themselves online. Once information is shared in cyberspace, it becomes part of a person's digital footprint. Unfortunately, if this information lands in the wrong hands, it can compromise one's personal safety, finances, or mental health. Communication in the digital world should be speedy, interesting, and fun, but it should not result in the exposure of sensitive information. People should think ahead and proceed with caution in order to protect their information and safety.

Profile Dangers

On social networking sites, people can post art, poetry, songs, photos, updates, and—most revealing of all—personal profiles. Many sites give people an introductory page on which to describe themselves and their interests. Young people must be extremely careful about what they share on this page. Full names, birth dates, names of siblings, parents' and grandparents' names, and home addresses—this is all information that should not end up in

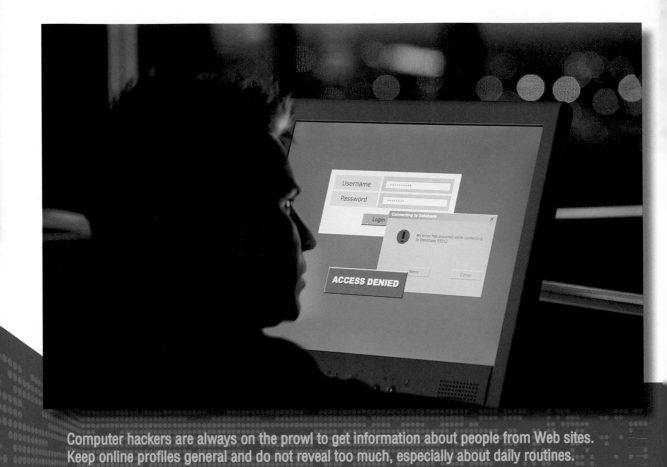

Computer hackers are always on the prowl to get information about people from Web sites. Keep online profiles general and do not reveal too much, especially about daily routines.

a profile on any Web site. In addition, young people should not reveal any information about their daily routines and schedules, such as which school they attend, which school bus they take, or where they go after school. Giving out this information makes it easy for identity theft to occur. Even more worrisome is that someone can use others' personal information to follow, stalk, or harass them.

Personal profile information may be intended for close friends only, but even if you choose to share your profile only with friends, hackers are not deterred. They can get into sites through back doors and steal information.

File   Edit   View   Favorites   Tools   Help

A TATTERED TWITTER

A Tattered Twitter

As more digital devices are invented, everyone's digital footprint grows larger. New worlds of communication are created. With each of these new conveniences come new responsibilities, risks, and potential digital missteps.

A Mesa, Arizona, man believes that his tweeting during a vacation might have tipped off burglars who wanted to rob his house. Using Twitter, he gave some two thousand friends and business associates real-time updates on his road trip. When he arrived back in Mesa, his home had been burglarized. Though there was no proof that tweeting played a role in the robbery, the victim was very suspicious. He owned an online video business and only his video-editing equipment was stolen. The robbers did not make off with any other consumer electronics devices in the home.

The more personal information you include in a profile, the more ammunition a hacker or identity thief has to exploit you. A hacker can contact you, claiming to be a friend of a friend, based on information you posted about yourself, including your school name, class schedule, and after-school activities. The hacker might try to gain your trust and then ask you to compare Social Security numbers or reveal other sensitive information.

Information can leak out more easily than you may think. For example, a friend may read your profile on a computer screen in a public place, such as a library or recreation center, and then forget to log off. Now anyone who passes by can see your information. Once this information is viewed, it can be used to piece together your life story.

Guarding Against Cybercrooks

In December 2008, security experts in London warned Internet users about a group of cybercriminals who were breaking into social networking accounts. The cybercrooks stole the personal information of thousands of people, as well as collecting their lists of friends. They sold this information to other criminals, who used it to send out spam e-mails that looked like they came from someone the recipient knew. The spammers made the e-mails sound very realistic. They would include something in the subject line that the familiar person might say, like "See a cute photo of my nephew, Jimmy." Sometimes the phony e-mails would include a picture that the hackers took from one of the victim's social networking sites. However, once opened, the message

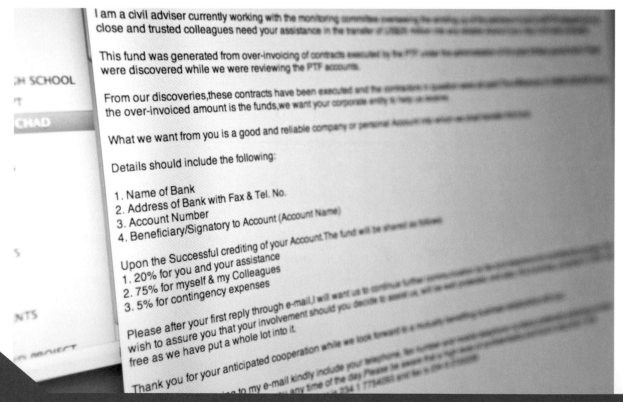

People should never respond to e-mails asking personal questions from someone they do not know. Many of these spam e-mails are designed to give cybercrooks access to private information.

would infect the computer with spyware. The software let hackers access private information like passwords, bank account information, and other personal data. The fake e-mail would ask people to send the photo along to their family and friends. If they did, the victims would unknowingly infect more and more computers. Then, the criminals collected private information from even more people.

Simple carelessness can lead to personal information getting out. Some social networking sites encourage members to acquire as many "friends" as possible, making the whole social networking experience a popularity contest. Sometimes people will give access to so-called "friends" they do not know, revealing private information—including blog entries and photos—to total strangers. One way to avoid this is to give access only to people you know in real life. Even then, it is still advisable to limit the information you put on the site. It is best not to post anything that could ever harm or embarrass you.

In addition, never exchange passwords with a friend. Passwords should be shared only with a parent or guardian. Be helpful to friends by not posting their private information on your site, and ask them to do the same in return. With digital devices providing such a free flow of information, it is important to be respectful of others' privacy.

Digital Exploitation and Sexting

There is never a good reason for anyone, especially someone who cares about you, to ask you to send explicit photos of yourself over the Internet or via a cell phone. Never consider complying with such a request. Sending suggestive pictures as a joke or as a way of flirting is dangerous. The photos remain in cyberspace forever, and you have no control over how they are used.

Sexting, the transmission of nude or sexually explicit photos via texting, is an abuse of digital communications. Law enforcement is cracking down heavily on the practice. Those who participate in it are actually committing a crime. People who send these photos can be charged with distributing pornography.

Sending suggestive photos is a dangerous way to use digital communications. The pictures can remain in cyberspace forever and hurt a person's reputation.

Those who receive them can be charged with possession of pornography. If people in the photos are under eighteen years old, sexting constitutes child pornography and carries even more serious penalties.

Teenagers in several states, including New York, Pennsylvania, and Wisconsin, have been charged with serious crimes stemming from sexting. Sexting can result in a criminal record, get a person labeled as a sexual predator, and get someone expelled from college or fired from a job. Anyone who uses digital communications should be concerned about sexting or any transmission of suggestive material. It violates a person's privacy and puts people at risk.

| File | Edit | View | Favorites | Tools | Help |

PROFILE TIPS

Profile Tips

To create a safer social networking profile, and one that will protect your digital footprint, try the following tips:

- Create a screen name with a positive persona, but one that still keeps your real identity secret. Consider making your screen name gender neutral for additional safety.
- Think critically about how you fill out the profile form. List positive role models, activities, and hobbies. However, do not include locations or schedules.
- Use the site's privacy settings to share information only with friends.
- Agree to be friends only with people you know personally offline. Don't give strangers access to your profile.
- Keep your location vague.
- Choose photos selectively. Don't post photos that show you or your friends violating school or family rules or breaking local laws.

Sexting is considered a form of sexual exploitation. It exposes people to ridicule and can be used to demean another person. In 2008, high school senior Jessica Logan, who lived in the Cincinnati area, committed suicide after an ex-boyfriend sent a nude picture of her to his friends in seven area high schools. The harassment and bullying that followed was too much for the young student to handle.

The National Center for Missing & Exploited Children reports that 51 percent of girls who sent out revealing photos of themselves were pressured by a boy to do so. Cosmogirl.com reported that, on an annual basis, 25 percent of the child victims of online pornography initially sent revealing pictures of themselves to someone they thought they could trust.

Gossip is often hurtful, yet people pass it along anyway, regardless of whether it is true or not. These photos are passed along the same way, without concern for whom they might hurt. The good news is that these problems can be avoided. Photos are a part of your digital footprint that you can control simply by not clicking the "send" button.

Overall, the most valuable tool in the digital world is good judgment. Managing a digital footprint takes some work and a measure of common sense. There is a great deal that can be done to shape the content of a digital footprint. Much of the information that people wish was not publicly displayed online often winds up there because they posted it themselves.

TEN GREAT QUESTIONS

TO ASK A COMPUTER SCIENCE TEACHER

1 How can deleted information be retrieved from a computer?

2 How can a hard drive be formatted, yet not have everything erased from it?

3 How can people know for sure that all important data has been completely erased from a computer that they want to sell or donate?

4 If a person brings a computer in for repair, can a technician legally look at the data on that computer?

5 If something is posted on the Internet, can someone figure out everywhere it has appeared?

6 Can someone find out what Web sites a computer user has visited, even if the Internet history has been deleted from that computer's browser?

7 Should people store passwords in their computers? Why or why not?

8 Can people be legally forced to turn over their personal computers or other digital equipment to law enforcement?

9 Are people responsible for things others post using their computer?

10 What privacy rights do people have if they are using a computer supplied by a school or workplace?

Chapter 4

Taking Charge

elebrities hire well-paid agents, public relations professionals, and lawyers to safeguard their public images and privacy. These professionals make sure that malicious rumors and unfounded stories are caught early, rooted out at the source, and replaced with correct information. They also try to keep some aspects of these famous people's lives out of the public eye.

Like these high-profile personalities, people everywhere should be concerned about the information that circulates about them in public. An online reputation can play such a significant role in a person's future that it is essential to properly craft, plan, develop, and manage this entity known as a digital footprint. A number of skills are necessary in order for people to use digital communications properly and in a way that will portray them in a positive light.

Do Your Research

It is important to learn as much as possible about any Web sites, including social networking sites, before sharing any personal information on them.

People in the public eye guard their reputations very carefully. This is something that all people should do, especially when they are online.

Certain Web sites may have long histories, good reputations, and credible track records. Even so, a great deal of information is being entrusted to an unseen source. As a result, it is a good idea to check out Web sites thoroughly. If necessary, ask a trusted person, like a parent or teacher, for help.

While Web site members are not usually asked to post a phone number or address for all to see, people might have to supply this information in order to sign up to use a site. That means the site sponsor is collecting information and, in turn, expanding your digital footprint or dossier.

The Privacy Statement

The Web site's privacy statement is one piece of information that should be read closely and thoroughly understood. Prospective site users should take it as a huge warning sign if a Web site asks for personal information but offers no written privacy policy. In that case, users should go no further. A privacy statement is similar to a consumer's bill of rights for the Web. The privacy statement should make it clear what information the Web site sponsors intend to collect and how they plan to use it. Reputable sites will give those who are signing up a choice about whether they will allow the site to collect and use the personal information in question.

Mark Zuckerberg, the chief executive officer of Facebook, held a press conference in 2010 to outline new privacy controls for the popular social networking Web site.

A Web site's privacy statement should specify the type of security the site uses to protect the personal information provided by members. Web security measures are designed to prevent information from falling into the wrong hands, being lost, or being altered without authorization. In addition, members should know how to access their personal information to check for accuracy and make any necessary corrections or updates.

Keep in mind that information provided to one site may be passed on to other connected sites. Privacy statements should cover how information is passed from one site to another when users click on a link. Many Web sites have working business relationships with other companies and share user information with those companies. Web sites must let users know information is being disclosed, explain how the other companies will use this information, and reveal whether the companies have agreed to keep the information confidential. The privacy statement must give contact information for the site and specify how the site uses cookies to track people's activities.

If a site fails to abide by the terms of its privacy statement and personal information about a user leaks out, the Federal Trade Commission (FTC) can take action against the site. In some cases, action can be taken on a state level as well.

Controlling Your Information

Web sites should also explain how users can limit their visibility. For instance, on Facebook, users can choose a setting to prevent their profiles and friend lists from coming up in a general Internet search, such as on Google. Similarly, photos on Flickr are available for everyone to see and can turn up in a variety of places in cyberspace unless the user who posts them selects the proper privacy settings.

People signing up to become a member of any Web site should also learn how information can be deleted if they should decide to deactivate their membership. On Facebook, for instance, when people decide to drop their membership, a simple deactivation does not remove the information they have posted on the site. Pictures, data, friend lists, hobbies—everything ever posted—remains there forever unless the user takes more extensive steps to eradicate the information. The way to do this is listed on Facebook, but many people think that simply deactivating an account will cause the information to be deleted automatically. It will not.

Using Chat Rooms, Newsgroups, and Mailing Lists

Many social networking sites provide chat rooms, or live online discussion groups. The Web site should explain how a user's identity is protected in any chat room it runs and who has access to each chat room.

File   Edit   View   Favorites   Tools   Help

THE BEST DEFENSE

The Best Defense

People should check what is being said about them online and make sure that any misstatements are corrected or removed. People can monitor their online presence by Googling themselves, or entering their own name in Google. They can also use tools like MonitorThis and Google Alerts to keep track of their digital footprint. If they find something online that is incorrect or that they want removed, they must act quickly before it is passed along.

The first step is to ask the party who posted it to remove it. If that does not work, there are companies that specialize in protecting people's reputations online. Called reputation defenders, these companies are in business to protect a person's image. They manage online reputations and try to protect a person's privacy. Besides offering monitoring services, these companies help people remove false, hurtful, embarrassing, and incorrect information that has made its way onto the Internet. Reputation defenders have taken the old adage "All I have is my good name" into the digital age.

Keep in mind that participating in a chat room with strangers is a risky activity. Chat rooms are generally unsupervised, and people using them could make violent, hateful, or other inappropriate comments. Reputable chat rooms for young people will provide a private network for a friends-only chat room.

Chat rooms keep records of messages sent while people are chatting, so it is best not to discuss any private matters in these chat rooms. The same is true of newsgroups and mailing lists. Before getting involved with chat rooms, newsgroups, mailing lists, or any online public forum, people should take the time to read the posts and make sure they are comfortable with what is being discussed and how the material is being presented.

Thinking Ahead

People can control much of their own digital image by being selective about what they put online. Besides keeping private matters offline, people should be thoughtful about what they do write online. For instance, people should be polite to others. Decency and consideration of others' feelings count online. Everyone should avoid:

- Making derogatory statements or racist and sexist remarks
- Using inappropriate language
- Making baseless statements
- Spreading rumors
- Bullying others
- Making references to abusing drugs and alcohol
- Writing about violence, taking revenge, or harming others
- Posting suggestive or risqué images

These kinds of posts reflect poorly on the person posting them, are hurtful to others, and usually remain part of a person's digital footprint for years to come. Even worse, such problems could be prevented if people thought more carefully about how they were using this technology.

One of the many steps people can take to create a positive digital footprint is to avoid viewing inappropriate Web sites.

Viewing inappropriate Web sites also becomes a permanent part of a person's digital footprint. All Web sites—including those that contain pornographic material, messages of hate, and references to illegal drugs—keep digital records of who visits the site. Your own computer records these visits as well. Part of a person's digital footprint, this information is often collected by police during an investigation. It is best to craft a digital footprint free of associations with these kinds of sites.

What can happen as a result of digital reputation slipups? The case of Mary Ellen Hause, a former part-time teacher's aide at Springboro High School near Dayton, Ohio, is a case in point. The forty-eight-year-old woman was pictured on Facebook in her home surrounded by three teenage cheerleaders—all holding liquor bottles. As a result of her bad judgment, she was arrested, charged with allowing underage drinking, and convicted. She was sentenced to thirty days in jail, given three years' probation, and fined $500.

Digital literacy is an important aspect of the digital communications boom. Positive digital footprints will open doors, while negative ones will slam those doors shut. Managing your online reputation has become as important as managing your reputation in the physical world. Like everything else in life, creating a positive digital presence takes effort. It is worth taking the time to protect your personal information and to create a digital footprint of which you can be proud.

GLOSSARY

blog An online journal or diary that someone makes available to others on the Internet; an abbreviation for Web log.

chat room An Internet site where participants can communicate and discuss topics in real time.

cookies Text files that collect and store information on a computer's hard drive.

cyberspace The online world of computer networks and electronic communication, especially the Internet.

derogatory Belittling, offensive, or insulting.

digital footprint The data trail, including personal information, created by a person's activities online.

dossier A file, including an online file, of personal information on someone.

identity theft The illegal use of someone else's personal information, usually to obtain money or credit.

ingenious Something characterized by cleverness or originality of invention.

malicious Exhibiting deliberately harmful behavior.

newsgroup An online discussion group that focuses on a particular topic or area of interest. Users can post messages to the entire group via e-mail or an electronic bulletin board.

party line phones Open central phone lines, often used by multiple customers in rural areas.

persona The public image or personality someone adopts when he or she is online.

pornography Obscene or sexually explicit writings, photographs, or drawings.

profile A person's description of himself or herself on a Web site.

prospective Possible.

risqué Verging on indecency.

smartphones Cell phones that, in addition to making voice calls, can run software, play media, and connect to the Internet.

social networking The use of a Web site to connect with friends or people who share personal or professional interests. The sites usually have interactive features, such as personal blogs, discussion boards, and chat rooms.

spyware Software installed on people's computers without their knowledge that tracks computer use and creates pop-up ads. Spyware can damage the computer and facilitate identity theft.

unblemished Flawless or without mistake.

viral Spread from person to person on the Internet or by e-mail.

FOR MORE INFORMATION

Federal Trade Commission (FTC)
600 Pennsylvania Avenue NW
Washington, DC 20580
(202) 326-2222
Web site: http://www.ftc.gov
The FTC focuses on Internet safety and privacy concerns, as well as many
other areas related to consumer interests. The FTC has a great deal of
information to help protect children and adults online.

Information and Privacy Commissioner (IPC) of Ontario, Canada
2 Bloor Street East, Suite 1400
Toronto, ON M4W 1A8
Canada
(416) 326-3333
Web site: http://www.ipc.on.ca/english/Home-Page
The IPC works to protect personal privacy and call awareness to the issue.

Internet Education Foundation
1634 I Street NW, Suite 1100
Washington, DC 20006
(202) 638-4370
Web site: http://neted.org/about
This nonprofit organization helps to promote safety and protect privacy on
the Internet.

Office of the Privacy Commissioner of Canada
112 Kent Street, Place de Ville
Tower B, 3rd Floor
Ottawa, ON K1A 1H3

Canada
(613) 947-1698
Web site: http://www.priv.gc.ca/index_e.cfm
This government office advocates privacy rights for Canadians and looks
    into complaints about privacy violations.

Pew Internet & American Life Project
1615 L Street NW, Suite 700
Washington, DC 20036
(202) 419-4500
Web site: http://www.pewinternet.org/Reports/2007/Digital-Footprints.aspx
This nonprofit organization presents information on how the Internet impacts
    everyday life, from schools to the workplace and beyond.

Society for New Communications Research (SNCR)
266 Hillsdale Avenue
San Jose, CA 95136
(408) 266-9658
Web site: http://sncr.org
This nonprofit foundation studies the latest developments in communications.
    It also helps to establish standards for new areas of communications.

Web Sites

Due to the changing nature of Internet links, Rosen Publishing has developed
an online list of Web sites related to the subject of this book. This site is
updated regularly. Please use this link to access the list:

http://www.rosenlinks.com/dil/mydf

FOR FURTHER READING

Cindrich, Sharon. *A Smart Girl's Guide to the Internet: How to Connect with Friends, Find What You Need, and Stay Safe Online* (Be Your Best). Middleton, WI: American Girl Publishing, 2009.

Cornwall, Phyllis. *Super Smart Information Strategies: Online Etiquette and Safety* (Information Explorer). Ann Arbor, MI: Cherry Lake Publishing, 2010.

Engdahl, Sylvia, ed. *Online Social Networking* (Current Controversies). Farmington Hills, MI: Greenhaven Press, 2007.

Fodeman, Doug, and Marje Monroe. *Safe Practices for Life Online: A Guide for Middle and High School.* Eugene, OR: International Society for Technology in Education, 2009.

Harris, Ashley Rae. *Txt Me L8r: Using Technology Responsibly* (Essential Health: Strong, Beautiful Girls). Edina, MN: ABDO, 2010.

Haugen, Hayley Mitchell, and Susan Musser, eds. *Internet Safety*. Detroit, MI: Greenhaven Press, 2008.

Keene, Carolyn. *Identity Revealed* (Nancy Drew: Girl Detective). New York, NY: Aladdin Paperbacks, 2009.

Lester, Brian. *R U In? Using Technology Responsibly*. Edina, MN: ABDO, 2011.

Mitra, Ananda. *Digital Communications: From E-mail to the Cyber Community* (The Digital World). New York, NY: Chelsea House, 2010.

Mooney, Carla. *Online Social Networking* (Hot Topics). Detroit, MI: Lucent Books, 2009.

Sandler, Corey. *Living with the Internet and Online Dangers* (Teen's Guides). New York, NY: Facts on File, 2010.

Selfridge, Benjamin, and Peter Selfridge. *A Teen's Guide to Creating Web Pages and Blogs*. Waco, TX: Prufrock Press, 2009.

Woog, Adam. *Mark Zuckerberg, Facebook Creator* (Innovators). Detroit, MI: KidHaven Press, 2009.

BIBLIOGRAPHY

Berkman Center for Internet & Society at Harvard University. "Enhancing Child Safety and Online Technologies: Final Report of the Internet Safety Technical Task Force." December 31, 2008. Retrieved January 27, 2010 (http://www.wiredsafety.org/resources/pdf/2009_isttf_final_report.pdf).

Bissonette, Aimee M. *Cyber Law: Maximizing Safety and Minimizing Risk in Classrooms*. Thousand Oaks, CA.: Corwin Press, 2009.

Carlson, Linda. *Internet Safety & Your Family*. Seattle, WA: Parenting Press, 2008.

Cavoukian, Ann. "Youth Online—Beware of the '5 Ps' When Using Social Networks: Focus!" November 5, 2009. Retrieved February 8, 2010 (http://www.ipc.on.ca/images/Resources/youthonline-madrid.pdf).

Danda, Matthew. *Protect Yourself Online*. Redmond, WA: Microsoft Press, 2001.

Durrani, Anayat. "'Sexting' Growing Trend Among Teens." GetLegal.com. Retrieved April 29, 2009 (http://public.getlegal.com/articles/sexting).

Gardner, Traci. "Creating a Safe Online Profile." IRA/NCTE, 2010. Retrieved March 17, 2010 (http://www.readwritethink.org/parent-afterschool-resources/activities-projects/creating-safe-online-profile-30306.html).

GetNetWise.org. "Get Privacy-Wise!" 2008. Retrieved January 25, 2010 (http://kids.getnetwise.org/safetyguide/privacy).

GetNetWise.org. "Online Safety Guide." 2008. Retrieved January 26, 2010 (http://kids.getnetwise.org/safetyguide).

Green Haven Press. *Internet Safety*. Florence, KY: Cengage Learning, 2008.

Gurak, Laura. *Cyberliteracy: Navigating the Internet with Awareness*. New Haven, CT: Yale University Press, 2003.

iKeepSafe.org. "Internet Safety News and Information: FTC's Net Cetera Gives Parents Tips to Help Children Be Safe Online." October 19,

2009. Retrieved January 26, 2010 (http://ikeepsafe.blogspot. com/2009/10/ftcs-net-cetera-gives-parents-tips-to.html).

Jennings, Charles, and Lori Fena. *The Hundredth Window: Protecting Your Privacy and Security in the Age of the Internet*. New York, NY: The Free Press, 2000.

Koch, Wendy. "Teens Caught 'Sexting' Face Porn Charges." *USA Today*, March 11, 2009. Retrieved March 15, 2009 (www.usatoday.com/ tech/wireless/2009-03-11-sexting_N.htm).

Lane, Carole A. *Naked in Cyberspace: How to Find Personal Information Online*. 2nd ed. Medford, NJ: Information Today, 2002.

MacDonald, Joan Vos. *Cybersafety: Surfing Safely Online*. Berkeley Heights, NJ: Enslow Publishing, 2001.

Negroponte, Nicholas. *Being Digital*. New York, NY: Alfred A. Knopf, 1995.

Palfrey, John G. *Born Digital: Understanding the First Generation of Digital Natives*. New York, NY: Basic Books, 2008.

Pew Internet & American Life Project. "Digital Footprints: Summary of Findings." December 2007. Retrieved January 26, 2010 (http:// www.pewinternet.org/Reports/2007/Digital-Footprints.aspx?r=1).

PRWeb.com. "Colleges and Universities Adopt Social Media to Recruit and Research Potential Students; Outpace Corporate Adoption of New Communication Tools and Technologies." January 20, 2009. Retrieved February 10, 2010 (http://www.prweb.com/releases/2009/01/ prweb1886224.htm).

Ribble, Mike. "Nine Elements: Nine Themes of Digital Citizenship." DigitalCitizenship.net. Retrieved January 26, 2010 (http://www. digitalcitizenship.net/Nine_Elements.html).

SafeKids.com. "Child Safety on the Information Highway." 2007. Retrieved January 24, 2010 (http://www.safekids.com/child-safety-on-the- information-highway).

SafeKids.com. "Facebook Privacy." Retrieved January 24, 2010 (http://www.safekids.com/facebook-privacy).

SafeTeens.com. "Social Web Safety Tips for Teens." 2007. Retrieved January 24, 2010 (http://www.safeteens.com/safe-blogging-tips).

SafeTeens.com. "Teen Sexting Tips." April 2009. Retrieved February 8, 2010. (http://www.safeteens.com/teen-sexting-tips).

Stein, Richard Joseph, ed. *Internet Safety* (The Reference Shelf, vol. 81, no. 2). New York, NY: The H. W. Wilson Company, 2009.

TeensHealth.org. "Protecting Your Online Identity and Reputation." 2010. Retrieved January 25, 2010 (http://teenshealth.org/teen/school_jobs/bullying/online_id.html#).

Treacher, Toby. "Facebook Privacy Settings 2010." DigitalParents.org. Retrieved March 26, 2010 (http://www.digitalparents.org/facebook-privacy-settings-2010).

Volonino, Linda, and Reynaldo Anzaldua. *Computer Forensics for Dummies.* Hoboken, N.J.: Wiley Publishing, Inc., 2008.

Willard, Nancy E. *Cyber Safe Kids, Cyber Savvy Teens: Helping Young People Learn to Use the Internet Safely and Responsibly.* Somerset, NJ: Jossey-Bass, 2007.

WiredKids. "STOP Cyberbullying: Cyberbullying—What It Is, How It Works and How to Understand and Deal with Cyberbullies." Retrieved February 1, 2010 (http://www.stopcyberbullying.org/index2.html).

WiredSafety.org. "Internet Safety: Internet 101—Blog and Diary Web Sites." Retrieved January 27, 2010 (http://www.wiredsafety.org/internet101/blogs.html).

Workman, Lisa. "Does Your Family Know How to Be Safe on the Internet?" iKeepSafe.org, January 2, 2007. Retrieved January 25, 2010 (http://www.ikeepsafe.org/iksc_about/news/?action=display_article&article_id=113).

INDEX

About the Author

Robert Grayson, an award-winning former daily newspaper reporter, has also written articles for numerous business publications and Web sites. His published pieces have profiled corporate leaders and spotlighted the latest technology, innovations, products, marketing, and public relations trends in business, industry, and commerce. In addition, he has written books for young adults on various topics, including network engineering, the FBI and cybercrimes, and the FBI and national security.

Photo Credits

Cover, pp. 1 (left), 13 Fuse/Getty Images; cover, pp. 1 (second from left), 19 Jupiterimages/Comstock/Getty Images; cover, pp. 1 (second from right), 5, 28 Hemera/Thinkstock; cover, pp. 1 (right), 24 James Lauritz/Digital Vision/ Getty Images; cover (background), interior graphics © www.istockphoto.com/ suprun; p. 8 Chris Jackson/Getty Images; p. 10 Tetra Images/Getty Images; p. 16 Michael Caulfield/WireImage/Getty Images; p. 21 Jupiterimages/ Photos.com/Getty Images; p. 26 Stockbyte/Getty Images; p. 33 Valerie Macon/Getty Images; p. 34 Kim White/Getty Images; p. 38 Joe Madeira/ Stockbyte/Getty Images.

Designer: Nicole Russo; Editor: Andrea Sclarow; Photo Researcher: Amy Feinberg